Daleswoman, Shepherdess and Pilgrim

Poems of Kate Rhodes

I am a life-long admirer of T.S. Eliot, Philip Larkin and W.H. Auden, and I really thought your poem came into their class

Letter from Tony Bridge, dean of Guildford, on receiving a poem about his cathedral after she visited it in 1985

Daleswoman, Shepherdess and Pilgrim

Poems of Kate Rhodes

THE CHOIR PRESS

First published in the United Kingdom in 2025 by
The Choir Press

ISBN 978-1-78963-575-1

© Cover image: Brandon C. Yen.

© Introduction: Peter Dale

Contents

Introduction

Like so many of her age and generation and background, Kate Rhodes would have encountered her first poetry in the verses of hymns ... and those first impressions remained with her in some measure all her long writing life. There is a simplicity of form(s), clarity and directness of communication – a messaging indeed – and a life-long subjectivity that connects her little *I* to the vastness of the infinity she apprehended around her.

There are broadly four phases, moods and contexts in her work. The first is a group of poems concerned with Central Africa where she was teaching between 1960 and 1964. It is the subjects – landscapes, lives, mores – rather than literary mannerisms, which dominate in poems of impeccable but unobtrusive prosody, simple structure and close observation. These are sensitive postcards, but shot through with a sympathetic intelligence which marks them out from mere snapshots – something of the eye of a journalist to be sure but also a precision and a thoughtful honesty that sets them apart, at least a little, from the type. The ruthlessness of African sun, its sheer 'terror', eclipses even the penetrating stare of a Greek Apollo, and almost the light of her own God whose 'quaint kindliness [only] glimmers in traceried glass' ('To the Sun of Africa', p. 1), remembered but almost replaced here by this pitiless, ineluctable light.

Kate was enormously sensitive to light (sometimes, I suspect, aching to spell it with a capital L), and then to its transmission ... especially through the eye, through the air, through glass. So much so that it comes as no surprise that a second group of poems is concerned very closely with that very thing, glass: clear glass, stained glass, in Bolton Priory (where she was an official, and surely singularly well-informed, guide), and then in York Minster. It is indeed glass which supplies the bridge between the terrestrial and the spiritual – a feat performed by 'God the glazier' but enabled by the very medium itself. The tone of these poems is variously rhapsodic, homiletic, witty. In one of the best of this considerable group – 'The Glazier's Night-Prayer', p. 15 – she imagines a mediaeval glazier going to heaven but asking for a special dispensation whereby he might still have his work-bench and tools and – though it is only God, of course, who 'makes all things new' – he (the glass-maker) might at least make heaven's 'glassy sea' more beautiful still with a dash of the old, the 'very old', in the form of colours 'mellowed by time', in the form of 'diapered blue, with gold and red'. This man proposes to give God a lesson in pigmentation, a lesson in seeing things through the eyes of a painter – Turner probably. The cheerful cheekiness and the dialogic manner recall George Herbert's conversations with his God three hundred years earlier, but through the rhapsodic glass of a visionary Traherne who saw, even in the most mundane of things, evidences of light trailed from the 'hem of God'.

In the poems written in her 50s – and she helping out at the farm of Cecil and Betty Hammond below Parcevall Hall – Kate engaged still with heaven but not now in the religious abstract. Now it was the capriciousness of the weather, the sound and sight of the skylarks and lapwings, the seasonally shifting textures of the skies above her that intimated a larger world above and beyond. Her feet are earthed ... in the turf of the hillsides, in mud sometimes, in slurry, stoniness. There is a realism and candour here, and a very individual voice. There is, moreover, a liberation in the form of her looser lines and in writerly adventures away from the domesticities of Georgian rhyming. The work moves from accomplished verse into convincing poetry. There is fresh energy and conviction in the (generally shorter) pentametrical lines and the vividness of the imagery. In 'Working Dog', p. 16, the almost exact synchronicity and complicity between animal and shepherd is not so much observed as enacted. It is

My finger on the trigger of her will
that governs what happens. The success of the fetch is embodied in
the collusion and cohesion of the dog

Thrusting her nose into my teasing palm,
Not slavishly, but with a comrade's kiss.

In 'February Fothering', p. 18, and other poems too, a local pastoral idiolect and dialect creep in, but with a light hand. *Fothering* (loading a wagon with hay and dragging it out to the sheep in late winter before the grass begins to grow again). *Tup* (both the ram himself and the process of impregnating the ewes). *Spained* (weaned). *Cobbed* (old, queer). There is, moreover, a faithfulness and earthiness in the observation: gravid ewes are those whose

… flanks swell with promised lambs
Like panniers, swinging low …

The biblical *thou*'s and *dost*'s of the earlier poems synchronise now with the real voices of Yorkshire men and women, as indeed they still do. And that sort of overlapping and correspondence between Kate's Christian vision and her quotidian employments on the farm are mirrored again and again in simple but telling correspondences between material things. There are synchronicities and correspondences that simultaneously (but gently) shock, and then convince and delight. In lines such as

Bunched sheep flow down the hillside like stormwater
Pouring down gullies in a torrent of frantic hooves

(from 'The Gathering', p. 25) the simile itself and its topographical precision ring true — both locally and universally. They authenticate the experience. The absence of sentimental pastoral postures convinces too — in 'Teeswater Tup in Spring', p. 17, the randy droop of the ram's nether lip and the 'skull battered bloody in a hundred fights' have no truck with the soft toys of nursery rhymes or the poetic dictions of fleecy clouds. But the hinterland and backdrops of the poems are peopled still with the biblical: one night in lambing time when the blizzard had 'dredged layer on layer of sifted snow', there is joy of course over the 'score' of successful births but sorrow too over the two deaths that also occurred that night, the 'two lambs, like yellow smears, apart and cold', laid out on 'a trampled ring of [bloodied] snow' ('Dead Lambs', p. 20), and you sense the presence not only of a careful sheep farmer but also of a Good Shepherd to whom the loss of even one sheep is more compelling than the safety of the ninety-nine secure in the fold.

Kate's most read, most revered poet was Wordsworth. She had an extraordinarily copious memory of lines, and a deep understanding. Yet you would hardly have known that – apart from the coincidence of pastoral moods – from the poems she had written so far. In the work of her very old age the connection becomes clear, but not before. Or not really. In these late effusions, however, you catch more and more of her lodestar ... when you look and listen carefully to what she wrote. There are some Wordsworthian allusions and references here and there, as in the poem 'Shadows' (not included here) where a skater, carried away by vertigo and finding the world – not him – hurtling by, remembers that famous early episode of *The Prelude*. Much more important than these occasional local moments, there is a thorough-going – and very Wordsworthian – collision of abstraction (beauty, fear, aspiration, continuity etc.) with materiality (for example, the 'common earth's stubborn solidity' as the observed context of a harebell's 'insubstantial loveliness' (p. 28).

Most of all, though, it is in the last poems that we find a moving out of and beyond the conventionally religious into the restlessly numinous. At her best this is what bespeaks and, indeed, reflects Wordsworth. In these poems only the natural world is taken *prima facie*: the rest is imaginative construction, re-construction, and bridge-making metaphor. Wordsworthian too perhaps is a series of poems apostrophizing particular flowers – pinks, phlox, harebells – but there is nothing fey or merely pretty about the way the poet examines them, treats them. Expect instead to find concatenations, clusters, of half-heard internal (half) rhymes ('despair' ... 'drear' ... 'year' ... 'fair', in 'The Reproof', p. 31); alliterations, so far from being merely conventionally decorative that sometimes they are more like intentionally violent expressive gobstoppers than the aural button-holes that weaker poets deliver: for example, this view of landscape contaminated by litter and 'plastic picnic cups'. There is a combative edge to poems such as 'The Reproof' (with its markedly Herbertian title). There's a sense too of foreclosing mortality – not exactly minatory but certainly admonitory, fused as it sometimes is with astonishing imagery, as when the poet notices that at dusk … 'hills slide up the sun' ('Shadows') There's an ecstasy in 'Winter Solstice', p. 29 – learnt from G.M. Hopkins perhaps, but earned here and won; shown not merely told – when, after a dreary, lightless winter she calls down benediction upon the sky in the east because it is 'ready' and

> A golden dawn of aconites awaits,
> Alert and confident, the call to rise
> And put to shame our joyless fantasies.

If Wordworth was Kate's favourite poet, Tallis was her favourite composer. She loved his long, almost pulseless (bar-less) lines and textures, and the sense of time suspended that they induce. As she has it 'music can force the locks on the gates of heaven ('On Hearing Gluck's Dance of the Blessed Spirits', p. 36). The music taught her – or reminded her anyway – that it is those 'printless feet' and much looser lines that elude the trap of time, be it musically metronomic time or syllabically mensurated verse – the sort of clumsy, number-crunched stuff that she had no time for and our school syllabuses – she knew – are now full of. In her earlier poetry those plodding iambics and anapaests must have come to her so easily … almost automatically in fact. And it shows. But not in these last poems. And perhaps it was music in general and Tallis in particular that reminded her that poetry – the real thing – deals not so much with the comforts of absolute conviction as with less easy but more authentic 'deep, disquieting loveliness' ('Dance of the Blessed Spirits').

Kate Rhodes – no doubt a very skilful teacher of students studying poetry at A level in the schools in which she taught – could (and perhaps sometimes did) write plausible verses with one arm tied behind her back. Going through those motions – albeit with scrupulous and impeccable technique – could have been her second nature. At her best, however, she transcended all that and it was her own voice, her own versions and visions of 'deep disquieting loveliness' that come through to reward the careful reader.

She seems to have had a sense of this herself: a comprehensive set of her manuscripts was lodged with her solicitor. And she was right. These poems amply, generously survive her.

Peter Dale

To the Sun of Africa

(The Karoo semi-desert witnessed her first night in Africa,
in transit from the port of Cape Town to the interior)

◊ ◈ ◊

I first saw you rise over the grey Karoo,
And felt the apocalyptic dread of your coming:
For the sky turned to sheets of stainless steel, which shook
And rang to the beat of your striding under the earth;
And the crouched pterodactyl hills heaved in the quaking air,
And cried aloud with a solemn and primitive cry,
And I felt their backs ache, as they braced to receive your load.

Then a piece of horizon melted, like burning wire,
                    And you rose:
Not Apollo of Delos with music of golden lyres,
Not *my* sun, who peers over sycamore tops
To the echoing fluting of blackbirds and breathing of leaves —
But a whirling, triumphant and trumpeting anger of fire,
A blaze elemental, and red with most ancient of blood
That runs in the veins of the rocks and the lava-seamed hills.

                    And I forgot God,
That small, far-off figure in gold and stained garments of blue,
Whose quaint kindliness glimmers in traceried glass,
Or crucified, pale, in stone, in the Northern light;
                    And I worshipped you.

But I feared you, too;
Your scarlet lances leapt from the level east,
And I felt their needle-jabs, hot in the skin and the eye;
The shrivelling cell, the burn in the flesh, and the sway
Of the dizzying brain, the thought growing dazzled and faint,
And the flame of loved beauties grew pale in your terrible light,
                  And I think I hated you.

The white steel rods of your brilliance imprison me now;
I walk with veiled eyes, daring no second glance,
Or hide in cool rooms till your terror has trampled and gone.
                  Yet I know, now,
What lies at the springs of Creation, what harshness and strength
Underlie the soft broideries of Nature, the green and the rose.
That tenderness, bruised by a snowflake and torn by a breath,
Has *this* for renewing, this vigour, this loud brazen mirth,
Promethean brightness too fierce to be quenched by our folly:
Our love's apprehensions fade out in the face of your laughter;
A deep need for something too great to be loved is appeased —
                  I am glad I have seen you.

Clouds in Africa

◇◈◇

Africa has no need of landscape, now:

Eye-level sight must weary soon enough
Of this drear stuff, this grey, pale, meagre grass,
The stiff reiteration of these trees —
Flat-topped and faded with their leather leaves —
Far as the shallow veldt's vast rim of vacancy
Where sky binds thornbush in a brazen ring.

But there, at the edge, where hot airs swirl and stir,
Rises the first proud peak of summer cloud,
Breeze-billowed banner of the mountain-hosts
Who range their slow battalions out of sight,
Ready to lift white crests against the sky's
Great cycloramic curve of polished blue.

First a dense cloud-ball, like a folded rose,
Involved and centred, opens to disclose
Green glow-worm lightning flickering in its heart;
Then creamy heads curl in the liquid light,
And swinging shapes commingle to a mass
Crisp-textured as a bolt of wind-blown silk.

Tall, striding towers of o'er-toppling might
Plant their proud feet upon horizon's verge,
And elbow up into the thronging heights;
Their solid sharkskin flanks are silver-smooth,
Stretched folds distended by the swelling airs,
Heavy with heat and big with hanging showers.

Foreshortened as they pass above our heads,
They march across and down the western slope,
Their ponderous bases trailing brokenly,
Until they melt into the evening fire.

The last wisp lingers, like a scribbled sign,
Ink-splashed upon a wash of dusky red;
And in the after-glow remains one grave
Thumb-smudge of grey upon a stainless field.

I live here

(To her companions on a day's excursion in the Dales)

◊ ◈ ◊

Yes, I live here; this is my land.
My homecomings are to a porch as grey,
Stony and solid as those we pass by.
I wonder how well you could understand
What it means to awake, each April day,
To the northern curlew's wilderness cry?

My pillow's beneath such a crusty beam
Which binds my walls to my roof of slate;
My window is filled up with fellsides — like those.
I wonder if you could even dream
What it is to sleep while November's spate
Broils where my turbulent river flows.

Yet, I am aware, because you see
My land with a less habitual eye,
I glimpse old grandeurs in ghyll and scar.
A wonder, that you should revive for me
The spell of the uplands' gritstone sky!
My land, so beloved; so familiar.

Priory Bell

(At the consecration of a new bell-turret, with a bell,
on the restored tower of Bolton Priory church)

◇ ◈ ◇

Below the rain-blurred hills and muffling trees'
Encumbered wetness in this wind-blown June,
The small bell beats its quiet code of threes
And centuries dance upon the point of noon.

No shouting at the gate, no bugle blast;
This gentle-spoken herald of the King
Musters eight hundred years of prayerful past
By age-old, three-fold, gracious summoning.

Our Lady leans, with stars about her face,
Above our loud, assertive womankind:
Thrice-hailed as blest, obedient, full of grace,
By angel guest and angelus combined.

The triple Sanctus — awesome, breathless chime —
Still marks the lifted Host, the upheld Cup,
And, for an instant, as in endless time,
Earth, laid upon Christ's palm, is offered up.

The voice of the Beloved is still and small,
But resonant beneath the raucous din
Of treadmill life — a low and winsome call
To one, to that one only, to come in.

So, little bell, ring now and every year,
And guide the searching ones towards this place,
For in your treble plainsong they shall hear
The word of fellowship, and love and grace.

The South Windows of Bolton Priory Church

(On the last two of a series by A.W.N. Pugin telling the life of Christ)

◊ ◈ ◊

Agreed that mediaeval glass is peerless
And lovelier than the downy leaves of beech
In sunlit woods ablaze with their green flames,
Only a stickler for antiquity could fail
To sense his spirit's kindling at the sight
Of Pugin's windows in this slanting ray,
Speckling the stonework with a patina
Of stippled red and blue and gold and mauve,
As bright as dragonflies in summer pools,
Or rainbows in the spray of waterfalls.

Suffering
Harsh pattern, rigid line, metallic roses
In wheels like implements of hideous death,
Express the agony of soul and body
Of Christ and those who heard his final breath.
Here loneliness, betrayal, treachery,
The degradation, unimagined pain,
The tears and weakness of exhausted sorrow,
All taut and stretched like cords near breaking strain.

Glory
The royal purple, rich and right indeed
For final glory; violet edge of light
Beyond the which our eyes lose all perception
And revelation must abandon sight.

Four groups of men and women, upward gazing
At marvels high above this earthly floor,
Where reason passes into exultation,
And we accept, and promise, and adore.

The Five Fingers of God

(The Five Sisters window, in the north transept)

◊ ◈ ◊

In childhood, once upon remembered time,
I heard a tune, played on a flute, far off;
And in the clouds that solemnly passed by
Grew golden citadels with walls and towers,
Familiar, so that when the music ceased,
I wept for an incommunicable loss.

A student, once by Semerwater lake,
When chilly sunlight chased across the fells,
I saw the ripples in the shimmering reeds
Glitter with sudden silver urgency;
And my whole being sensed a presence there,
And for an instant crossed the edge of time.

In middle years, where the Zambesi pours
In one great, mile-wide, smoking cataract,
And ageless rainbows hover in the spray,
I heard, below the thunderous roar, a voice,
That called, and vanished with the vanishing foam,
As a white ibis plunges and is gone.

And later, from an antique harbour wall,
I gazed into the Aegean's limpid swell,
Where shoals of glimmering fishes paused and fled
Through sunlit greens and wavering lines of gold;
Till self-awareness slid into content,
And rested in a tranquil otherness.

O rich indeed, that four times in one life
My hand should brush the fingertip of God:
That which the poets dream and mystics seek.
How dared I then expect a further grace?
I thought my soul was aged, numb and blind,
Till angels stirred the quickening pool again:

For yesterday, five windows, like cool flames,
Grey as doves' feathers or Northumbrian seas,
Sprinkled with flecks of silver, red and blue,
Beckoned across the minster's echoing space;
I went, and was enfolded in their peace,
Handclasped by God's five fingers for a while.

The Mantle of Mary

(A hymn to the Blessed Virgin in the mediaeval manner,
on panel VIII 6 of the great east window)

❖ ❖ ❖

Was ever one
Since time begun
That made her mantle
Of the sun?

I saw a door,
A gate of glass,
And into paradise
Did pass.
I met a maiden
Walking there
Who wore the stars
Upon her hair.

The moon for footstool
Had she found
To guard her slippers
From the ground,
But from the shoulder
To the knee
Clothed in a cloak
Of sun was she.

Was ever one
Since time begun
That made her mantle
Of the sun?

The golden rays
Were ribbons rare,
The broideries
Both bright and fair,
In silks of day
And pearls of dawn,
Like dazzling drops
On Mayday morn.

She bore a babe,
Jesu, her joy;
A dragon dark
Did him annoy;
But she, to shield
Him from affright,
Sewed him a little
Shift of light.

Was ever one
Since time begun
That made her mantle
Of the sun?

To a little Lion, 600 years old

◊ ❖ ◊

Young lion, with the chubby, impish baby face,
What *is* it you've been up to?
Your innocent, rounded eyes, slewed to the left,
Under those quirked and anxious brows, suggest
To me that you're avoiding Someone's gaze.

Whatever it is you've done, you certainly
Enjoyed it! And you're relishing it still;
Witness the sauceboat smile which puckers up
Your cheeks, despite your guilty look; and that
Impudent tongue just longs to lick your chops,
Seeking the savour of your little crime.

Are you the lion from God's holy mountain,
Doomed to 'eat straw like the ox'?
And can you perhaps have taken a little nip
Out of that calf you're supposed to be friendly with?
Or is it expulsion you fear? Or just a lecture?
I don't think you're taking it very seriously.

I expect you know that God looks so awfully solemn
Because He's already working on the problem
Of flavouring straw with beef!

The Portrait

(The face of God the Father, South Transept west wall, 15th century)

◊ ◈ ◊

He must prepare to tread a daunting path,
Out to the furthest reach of art's perception,
Who would presume to paint the face of God.
For what can paint the light except the light?
God must both sit and charge the brush Himself.
And so He chose a painter upon glass
(Whose palette's bare until it is splashed with light)
And what the man, for brightness, could not see,
He showed him in the simple things of earth.

'Look', He said, 'at the lines in flowing water.
Look at the lines the swallows weave in air;
Look at the circles of the moon and planets;
Look at the shapes of leaves, the curls of fire.
These are the contours of My countenance'.

'The eyes, Lord?' asked the painter. 'Look', said God.

So he looked at the button eyes of trout and robins,
He looked at the soft brown eyes of gentle cows,
The eyes of young men, bright with resolution,
The old men's moist eyes with their drooping lids,
The glowing eyes of lover facing lover,
The eyes that search for truth and beauty still.
And all this knowledge, passion, love and strength
He spent on his masterpiece — the eyes of God.

'Lord, how to paint your mobile, anguished mouth?'
He cried, despairing. Gently, God bent down,
And kissed the glass, leaving the imprint plain.

A Resurrection Window

(To her mother, who died, a schizophrenic, aged 67)

◊ ◈ ◊

Iconoclastic wars and wanton fires
Leave noble windows scarred, deranged and dull;
So did the pinching harshness of your life
In the grimed city, scuffling with brutal winds,
Buckle and craze your soul till it became
The faintest outline in a senseless maze,
The leafless, tangled thicket of your mind.

In death there is, I think, a fiery bench
Where God dismantles us and cleans each part
(As do the glaziers I am bid to sing)
Setting us back, restored, in the ordered frame
Of the cartoon He drafted in conception.

And so, my mother, do I see you now,
Living, as thirty years before you died,
A shy girl still, with dark unruly hair
And wistful eyes, leading me by the hand
Through woodland, with cool bluebells in the shade;
A self-taught scholar, devotee of words;
A gentle wit, wise with instinctive knowledge;
A passionate heart, that craved the red wine of life.

Praise, then, to God the glazier, who invests
The mutilated with the comely flesh
Of a resurrection body, veined with light.
This window, re-installed in my heart's chantry,
Unfurls its scroll in bright calligraphy,
'Lux perpetua luceat eae'. Amen.

The Glazier's Night-Prayer

◊ ◈ ◊

Lord, when at length I reach the time
When I must golden ladders climb
Into the everlasting day,
Grant me a secret gallery, pray,
Where night is free to come and go,
That I may still see evening glow
And level shafts of daybreak pass
Through mellow panes of painted glass.

And, though Thou dost make all things new,
Keep me, I pray, a piece or two
Of fragile glazing, very old,
Diapered blue, with red and gold;
A workbench hid behind Thy throne,
Some lead and tools to call my own;
And may I set Thy glassy sea
With dappling colours, Lord, for Thee?

Working Dog

◊ ◈ ◊

My finger's on the trigger of her will,
And with the lightest pressure I can launch her
Swift as a falcon, with far-focused eye.

My falcon needs no jesses and no lure;
Her leash is a bond of trust, and she obeys
The ancestral duties of her loyal breed.

She vanishes over the harebell height
But I am easy, for she knows my will;
As mine, so hers, concentric on the task.

Soon the expected phalanx of horned heads
Breaks the horizon, and with managed speed
Sweeps down the hill to halt before my eyes.

Dancing with pride in her delighted skill,
She bounds beside me on the homeward drive,
Thrusting her nose into my teasing palm,
Not slavishly, but with a comrade's kiss.

Teeswater Tup in Spring

(Northern word for a ram)

◊ ◈ ◊

He skulks aloof, surly, with drooping lip,
Skull battered bloody in a hundred fights,
And greasy wool half-ripped from his tattered side.

His bitter, low-browed face seems unaware
That springtime's sweetest buds broke from his loins,
And meadows peopled by his gentle seed.

February Fothering

◊ ◈ ◊

Skylarks shrill in the roofless blue,
The cold, hard sun is bright,
Moorland grass is pallid gold,
Though the far hills are white.

Red tractor stands, piled high with hay,
The eager flock mills round,
And little straggling lines of sheep
Race up from lower ground.

From winding hillside trackways, hung
With hawthorns, broken-boughed,
They summon one another, with
Their dark tongues belling loud.

As heaps of fragrant hay are strewn
Along the sheltered wall,
The sheep run to and fro to seek
The sweetest bite of all.

They munch the brittle flower-heads
The stalks, still full and green;
Their teeth pluck out the clover-stems
Entwined in between.

The scents preserved from summer days
Breathe faintly in the cold;
The rustling mouthfuls whisper
As the packed swathes unfold.

The ewes' flanks swell with promised lambs,
Like panniers, swinging low;
They run with a heavy, laden gait,
Feeling their burden grow.

Larks and sun and lingering scents
Of meadows mown in June —
Such are the joys of fothering sheep,
When spring's expected soon!

Dead Lambs

◇◈◇

A night of blizzard, with a bright dawn after;
We ran with anxious haste to see the lambs
New-dropped in the hours of howling darkness.

All night, as the ice-grains peppered the window
And sky dredged layer on layer of sifted snow,
I'd thought of drenched ewe upon bitter child-bed,
Lambs thrust forth into shuddering air,
Opening their new-made eyes on shrieking blackness,
Groping for the teat through a tangle of snow-dagged wool.

Oh, miracle of the childlike voices
That sang through the frost to praise the day!
A score of lambs, like Eden's blossoms,
Had flowered on the whipped, black boughs of the storm!
One danced in the snow, for bliss of the sunlight;
Another, tucked warm by the wall,
And blanketed deep in his dam's draping mantle,
Slept milky and nodding and dreamt of the womb;
Some, prick-eared and curious, eyed us with pleasure;
All shone with a lustre of life.

But ah! There is blood in a trampled ring of snow —
Two lambs, like yellow smears, apart and cold,
Mouths wide as if still ready to expel
Their first, unwelcome gasp of sleety air;
Jet hooves, sheathed still in jelly of parturition,
Never to scamper at mother's throaty call;
Chill tongues that never pressed the warm, full teat;
And clouded eyes that briefly glimpsed the light
And closed again on night.

Not twenty breathing lambs on that bright morning
Could countervail the heartache of that sight.

Old Cadger

(The voice of her farmer friend Cecil Hammond.
Drafters: old sheep to be sold off because unlikely to winter. Spained: weaned.
Lower down: south. Cobbed: odd. Shedder: gate to be turned either of two ways)

◇ ◈ ◇

'Who's this that's nudgin' at mi backside, then?
Owd Cadger? Owt to 'a known it wad be thee!
Tha got thi name playin' them sooart o' tricks,
Noseyin' rahnd me fer a bit o' cake!
What's tha tryin' to tell me, then, owd lass?
Ah bet tha dussen't reckon much o' this,
Bein' penned up wi' a packet of owd drafters;
None of 'em looks much bottle at side o' thee.

Oppen thi gob an' let's inspect thi dentures:
Nay, damn! Tha's but one tooth left i' th' heead!
'S wuss ner Ah thowt. Ah don't know what to say.
Tha's fetched up two lambs ivver sin Ah kenned thee,
Kept track on 'em an' tanked 'em up reet weel;
One year tha 'ad a blind 'un, didn'ta?
An' nivver left it side till it were spained.
Tha's brokken-mouthed, but tha's i' rare good fettle;
'Appen Ah'd rue it if Ah parted wi' thee.

Can'st tek another winter, dosta think,
On th' sooart o' goin' that we hes up 'ere?
Or should Ah send thee packin' wi' this pen-full,
To softer country, mebbe, lower down,
Where tha mowt thrive a two-three year or more?

22

By, tha's a cobbed 'un, stuck there i' mi rooad,
Like tha kens gey weel what's goin' on!
Ah tell thee what — Ah'll leave th' gate oppen for thee
Into th' shedder, an tha can suit thisen
Whether tha stops wi' me or flits wi' them ...
Ah'll be reet chuffed if tha's i' th' mood to stay!

The Miracle

(Cecil wraps an orphan (gimmer) lamb in the skin of a stillborn, whose
mother adopts it. Trip: time. Capped: perplexed. Bunch: kick.
Brossen: overflowing. Gurgled up: encumbered.)

◊ ◈ ◊

'Tha's med a reight mess on it this trip, missis,
Lossin' a bonny newborn lamb like this.
Whativver notion got into thi noddle
To mek thee start to lick it at th' tail end,
When th' poor lile devil couldn't draw breath
For th' lump o' skin stuff clapped across his snout?
Ah'm capped at thee; a four-shear yowe, an' all.

Yer gurt daft brush! It's no good pokin' at it!
Tha could bunch it twice round th' croft – it weean't stir!
Nah! Don't look glum; Ah'll do summat about it;
Ah'll see if Ah can mek it go for thee.
Ah'll fetch mi whittle an' tek off 'is jacket
(While thou looks t'other way i' this tin o' cake) —
Ah reckon Ah've a gimmer lamb wad suit thee,
What's mum went down wi' th' illness t'other day.
'S a big un', but tha's brossen full o' milk;
Tha'll fetch it up an' mek a sheep out on it.

There now! — thi lamb is heckish gurgled up
I' th' little cardigan, but nivver mind;
If it does th' trick, we'll tek it off termorra'.
Go on then — talk to it an' fuss it up;
Tha's gotten th' lamb of th' year theer, tha knows!

Tha looks reight suited, now it's suckin' thee:
Ah bet thou thinks Ah've done a miracle!
Off wi' thee, then, down th' field, an' show thi mates;
Ah'll keep mi trap shut if tha claims it's thine!'

The Gathering

(Runner-up for the Yorkshire poetry prize 1984.
Cripple-hole: a low opening which sheep can only pass in single file)

◊ ◈ ◊

Bunched sheep flow down the hillside like stormwater,
Pouring down gullies in a torrent of frantic hooves,
And spilling out wide and shallow on open turf;
Cascading down screes with a foam of tossed fleeces and shale,
Spurting in jets from the cripple-hole choking their way.

Singly, they glide down the sheep-tracks like droplets on wire,
And submerge in the seething pool at the pasture gate,
Roaring with panic, and stirred by long-tongued dogs.
The lane is a river, swift-bobbing with rippling horns,
Till the grey tide laps quietly up on the shores of the farm.

Lamb Sale Day

◇◈◇

The huge red cattle wagon, three decks high,
Is moored like a liner at the farmyard gate.
Five minutes more, and she must sail with her
Three hundred passengers, now tightly penned,
Calling their loud, incredulous farewells
To the grieved sheep, who know the heavy score.

A signal given, the sloping gangway lowered,
An embarkation forced by men and dogs;
No time for a backward glance, lambs stream on board
Like swarming bees impelled into the hive.
The hatches closed and moorings cast adrift,
The wagon pulls away and gathers speed
Down the long hill and out into the road,
Glimpsed momentarily between the trees,
And then it vanishes and all is still.

Who weeps upon the quay to see them go?
The men turn in for breakfast, but for me —
I linger with the stunned and silent ewes
And share with them my tears of leave-taking;
For lambs I saw emerge into the light,
For hungry orphans butting round my knees,
For those whose need for tenderness and skill
Nullified pain of cold and weariness;
The innocent play along the sunset banks
Which turned Home Meadow into Holy Mountain.

Adieu, my lambs, as on some lowland farm
You learn to feed and grow and walk alone
With the strong limbs you nurtured on our hills;
Forgive the hurtful lesson of today:
That even shepherds cheat you at the last.

Harebells

◊ ◈ ◊

To see a harebell, even one, to me
Is something numinous. How can it be
Such insubstantial loveliness should rise
From common earth's stubborn solidity?

That filament of a stem, which makes the grass
Look clumsy — how came it that it broke
Through stiffened layers of hoof-marked, nibbled turf?
Nor snapped under sidelong blows of wind and rain?

That tiny bud, tight as a rolled umbrella,
With unimaginable skill unpacked
Diaphanous folds, without a crease or tear, —
Opened the delicate fabric as a bell

Brimful of sunlight, softly tinged with blue —
Ephemeral blueness of a frosty sky;
Haunting the eye and tightening the throat,
Hinting at worlds and presences unseen.

Winter Solstice

(As seen from the windows of her retirement home in Grassington)

◊ ◈ ◊

From Michaelmas till now, the rising sun
(A bright ball lost by rueful cherubim)
Has rolled inexorably away from us
Down and a-down the steep flank of that hill,
To drop, today, with almost audible thud,
Into that cleft where skylines intersect.

Just one more day, and would it — might it — slip
Beyond recovery? The ancient fear still haunts us:
An Arctic Night of darkness and unknowing;
The groping terror; frightened eyes that search
For glimmers of a day that never dawns,
And, worst of all, the shadow in the mind.

But Earth, bless her, is ready as she spins
To toss the bright ball back along its arc.
The flowers know this, of course, and even now
A golden dawn of aconites awaits,
Alert and confident, the call to rise
And put to shame our joyless fantasies.

Messages

◊ ◈ ◊

'Things for ever speaking' wrote the poet,
Referring to Nature — mountains, birds and trees.
Most of us, I'd say, know what he meant.
Lakes say 'Be still', crags bid us persevere,
Dodgem-ing ducklings plead for tenderness,
The peewit shouts, 'Cast care aside! Rejoice!'

The heavens declare the deity, and we
For aeons have scanned the sky's wide message-board
For counselling in clouds and constellations,
Zodiacal symbols, solstice sunrises,
Comets, eclipses — and the ominous glare
Of crimson dawns, the shepherd's weather warning.

A white bird quits the homeward-winging flock;
Makes for my window, keen and purposeful.
I hold my breath, half guessing at his errand —
A sudden swerve — he catches the evening sun —
Signals in luminous white and gold — and melts
In cloud, as foam-flecks melt upon the stream,
Leaving three words of solace: 'You are dear'.

The Reproof

◇◈◇

O Earth! Belovèd, open your eyes, lest we
Who watch beside your bed of sickness, yield
To blank despair, drear as these sunless skies
That weigh on us this year, like a dusky shroud,
Destined to be fair Nature's Doomsday dress.

Speak to us, Earth! Where are your vanished voices?
Grasshopper, cricket, cuckoo-bird and snipe?
Wildfire's throaty roar, tornado's scream,
Speak not of might or majesty but pain:
Pain we inflicted and, too late, deplore.

Your lacerations, where we dig and drill
Voraciously, we plug with nuclear waste
And plastic picnic cups; bulldozers bruise,
Tanks and tractors crush and suffocate,
And toxins sear the sap within the vein.

Return, Creator Spirit! Move anew
Upon the face of our polluted waters,
Our 'brown field' wastes and concrete wildernesses;
Restore the broken rhythm of the seasons
And plant a second Eden in the dust!

But He replied: 'All this is yours to see to.
Creation's 'Fiat' cannot be revised,
And Earth – like you — is irreplaceable.
Eden is out of bounds, until that Day
When Time gives place to an eternal Now.'

So ponder this, my soul, and weigh it well;
Who, amongst us, could be entrusted
To tend the fruit trees in a second Eden?

Ingle-nook, Parcevall Hall

(A Jacobean retreat-house in Wharfedale which she frequented)

◊ ◈ ◊

'Nook' is not the word; this massive gritstone arch
Carries the weighty chimney-breast and spans
The wide recess, the hearth-stone's roominess,
Where countless generations will have lingered
(The prosperous, the titled and the humble),
Held hands out to the fire, and gone their way.

Gritstone is sturdy stuff; its genesis
Primaeval, unimaginable pressure,
Transmuting silt into solidity.
Hammer and chisel, tools of sharpened steel,
Fashioned that curve and grooved the stones to fit,
Enduing mass with grace and symmetry.

Should the house fall, this surely would remain
Upstanding in the rubble, and become
(With castles, abbeys, antique dried-out harbours)
A poignant witness to an aspiration —
The gathered household, warming hands together;
The fireside focus, signifying *Home.*

Appletreewick

(On the cottage which she left in 2005)

◊ ◈ ◊

An outcrop of stone houses on a hillside,
Halfway between the shaggy upland pastures
(Where nagging winds might frighten them away)
And the dangerous, sportive beauty of the river,
Chatterboxing its rocks and tree-roots restlessly
And luring some to dream and some to drown.

The village street hangs between church and inn:
The first, diminutive, endearing, bright
With polish, flowers, and sudden Glorias
From roof-top blackbird's fervent ministry,
And slanting sunbeams peering through the panes.
The other, whitewashed, offers a wayside halt,
Benches and tables for mid-day hikers' break;
On summer nights, soft lights and distant laughter.

Look east, or west, or all ways: nothing else —
A scatter of farms and barns, but overall
Assuaging green to the horizon's edge.

Half-hidden cottage, part way up the hill,
Modestly tucked in, sideways to the road,
Facing its own walled garden's secret space,
Bird-hostelry. A giant laburnum tree
Cascading gold; and, later in the year,
The thud of windfall apples on the lawn.

I, long removed by age and frailty,
Heart-tethered ever to this tract of earth —
Base of belonging, home-ground of my soul —
Suffer the pain of alienation still;
The insistent pull of the unattainable
Return to Elysian sufficiency.

Tears

◈ ◈ ◈

My neighbour's aged cousin, in fireside chair,
Cradled the lamb upon his swollen knees,
One gnarled and mottled hand, with broken nails,
Tracing the crisp, warm curls of new-made wool,
The other cupping the small dome of the head.

The shepherd lad, shedding his boots at the door,
Had burst in, like a gust of moorland breeze,
And a voice to match, ringing with youthful pride.
'Grandad! What's tha think o' this un then?'
And placed the little creature on his lap.

'Aye lad, tha's reet enough — a bonny lamb.'
The pale eyes glazed, unfocussed, dreamily —
Then strove to hide the tears that sprang, unbidden,
Under the lids and down the furrowed cheeks,
While sobs, suppressed, convulsed and choked his voice.

I pitied then, and did not understand.
But now, when age enfeebles and retards,
My eyes can moisten when I recollect
The morning round, before the break of day,
The tumbling peewits and the curlew's plea,

The ewe's soft chuckling to her new-born lamb;
The first breath and the tiny sneeze that followed.
There is a passion in the shepherd's heart
That never fades — and only God can know
How my hands ache to hold a lamb again.

On hearing Gluck's 'Dance of the Blessed Spirits'

◇◈◇

Merely a breath, waylaid in a narrow flute,
Merely a tremor in the atmosphere
Throbbing against the membrane of the ear,
Conjures this music — yearning, interceding,
Love-longing with an ache for lost content;
Rising, sinking, straining, like the lark
Pleading her cause above the morning mist.

Music can force the locks on the gate of heaven.
It softens as it briefly ushers us
Into the gardens of Elysium.

A shimmer of stately figures, two by two,
Tread a graceful measure on printless feet,
In blissful concord, hand in tender hand,
Faces alight with love and hope fulfilled,
Glances and smiles of innocent gaiety.
We gaze and marvel, but anon we weep,
For there are faces here that we remember.

Beatitude and sorrow mingle strangely,
But both are exquisitely voiced within
This music's deep, disquieting loveliness.

The Climb

(In old age she recalls youthful pursuits, such as bell-ringing, and awaits death)

◊ ◈ ◊

The door slammed shut upon the winding stair —
Sole access to this lofty parapet.
No going back, no abseiling return,
So value the air and prospect while you may
(Though compass points seem now irrelevant).

Your breath would fail now on those distant hills;
Your feet would stumble on the woodland path.
Lean, and look down between the churchyard trees,
Where family and friends lie inaccessible,
Like books your fading eyesight cannot read.

The foothills of your climb lay in the church:
The 'hands uplifted', the 'uplifted hearts',
Inspired your questing soul to attempt the stair,
Past the ringing-chamber, silent now,
The ropes looped up, the sallies motionless.

Past the ponderous silence of the bells,
Waiting the call to mirth or mournfulness;
Past narrow, cobwebbed window-slits, until
A yielding door let in a flood of light,
And grateful feet stepped onto level space.

The spire's precarious height remains to climb,
By worn, uneasy footholds in the stone's
Relentless diminution as you rise.
The wind is cold and night is coming on.
Lastly, the finial's point affords no choice —

But letting-go and reaching for the sky,
Trusting that stronger hands than yours will catch
And free you from the mesh of fretful Time,
To find felicity and fellowship
With poets and shepherds in celestial fields.

Kathleen (Kate) Rhodes, 1929–2023

Kate was educated at Bolling Grammar School, Bradford, where she was Head Girl, and at Bedford College, University of London, where she graduated in English in 1951. She also gained a lifelong interest in Christian scripture and doctrine through the Youth Fellowship of Bradford Cathedral. After training at Hughes Hall, Cambridge, she taught at five successive schools, in three of which she was Head of English: Queen Margaret's School, Escrick Park, York (1952–7), Guildford Girls' High School (1957–9), Arundel School, Salisbury, Southern Rhodesia (now Harare, Zimbabwe, 1960–4), Surbiton Girls' High School (1964–5) and Skipton Girls' High School (1967–85). In 1977 she received a testimonial 'To the best form mistress in the world'. She later wrote: 'I was passionate to share my riches with my pupils and teach them not merely to know things but to think, to feel, to understand, to wonder'.

From 1965 to 1967 she was Assistant Warden at Parcevall Hall, a diocesan retreat house at Appletreewick in Upper Wharfedale. There she met the Hammonds of adjacent White House Farm, whom she helped as assistant shepherd from 1969 to 1998, the happiest time of her life. She was clerk to Appletreewick Parish Council from 1973 to 2003, living in the village from 1982; she also contributed to the restoration of Parcevall Hall gardens, as treasurer of the Friends. In retirement she became a local preacher, notably in the priory church at Bolton Abbey which she served as guide, housekeeper, bible-study leader and columnist of the parish magazine. A rector wrote: 'I admired her closeness to God'. Meanwhile she spoke on English poetry to many local societies, leading a literature group for the University of the Third Age. She gave her last talk to great acclaim at the age of 90, on poetry which she was too blind to read but knew by heart.

John Rhodes

www.ingramcontent.com/pod-product-compliance
Lightning Source LLC
LaVergne TN
LVHW041209080426
835508LV00008B/875